ARTIST TRANSCRIPTIONS®
GUITAR
NOTES & TAB

Transcribed by
JIM JOSSELYN
and
DAN TOWEY

THE **JOE PASS** COLLECTION

C000102377

Cover photo © 1997 Jimmy Katz/Giant Steps.
Photography assistance by Laura Coyle

ISBN 978-0-7935-6427-9

HAL•LEONARD®
CORPORATION
7777 W. BLUEMOUND RD. P.O. BOX 13819 MILWAUKEE, WI 53213

Visit Hal Leonard Online at
www.halleonard.com

Blues for Basie

By Joe Pass

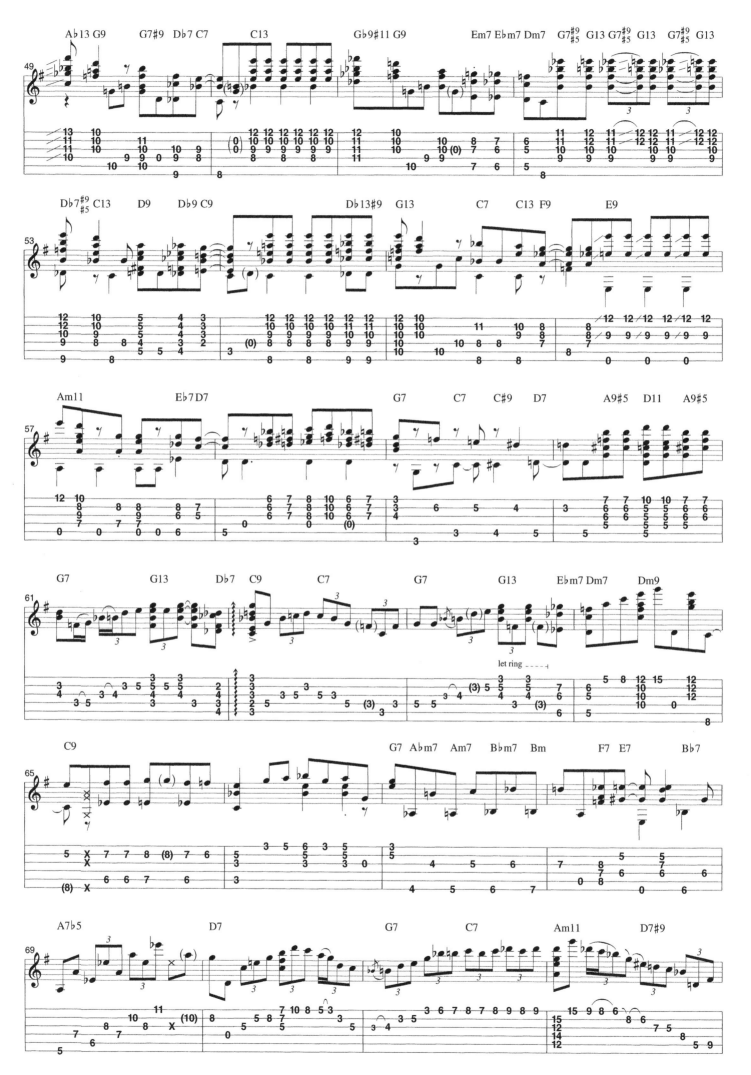

4

Blues for Hank

By Joe Pass

Available by Joe Pass on CD and cassette from:
Buster Ann Music, P.O. Box 9071, Marina del Rey, CA 90292,
and on the internet at www.beachnet.com/~bamusic/

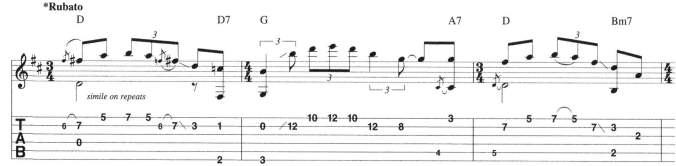

*Solo Gtr. Tempo fluctuates between 82 - 144 b.p.m.

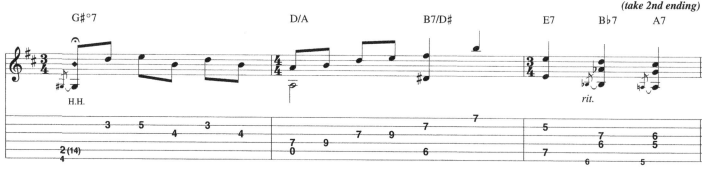

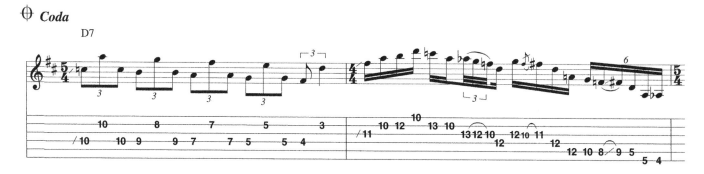

⊕ Coda

Cheek to Cheek

Words and Music by Irving Berlin

*Solo Gtr. tempo fluctuates between 120 - 176 b.p.m.

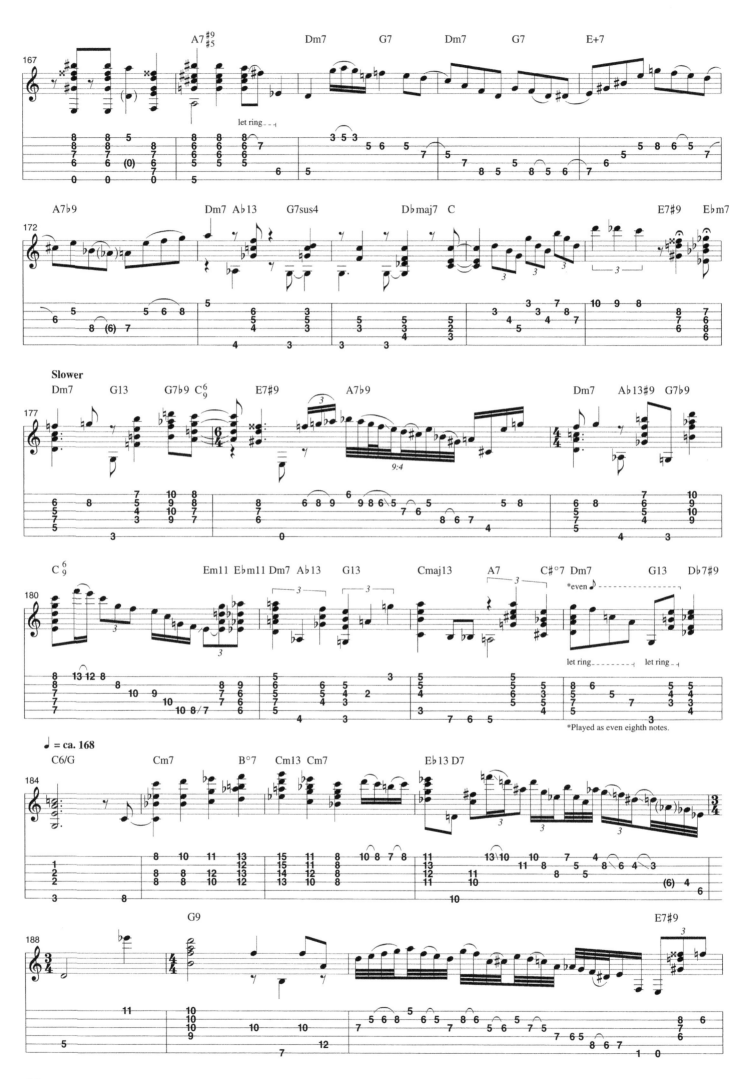

Dissonance #1

By Joe Pass

*Solo Gtr. - Tempo fluctuates between 110 - 144 b.p.m

Happy Holiday Blues

By Joe Pass

Available by Joe Pass on CD and cassette from:
Buster Ann Music, P.O. Box 9071, Marina del Rey, CA 90292,
and on the internet at www.beachnet.com/~bamusic/

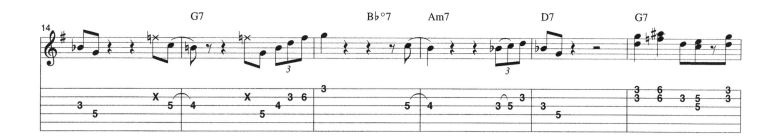

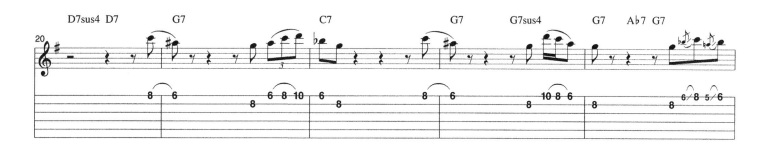

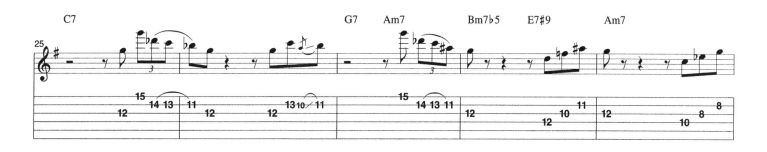

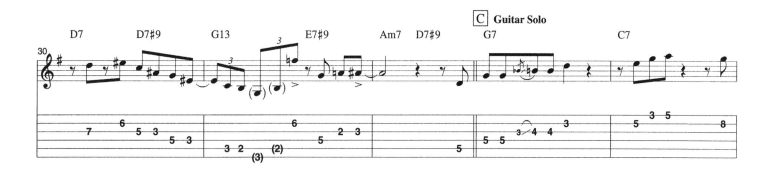

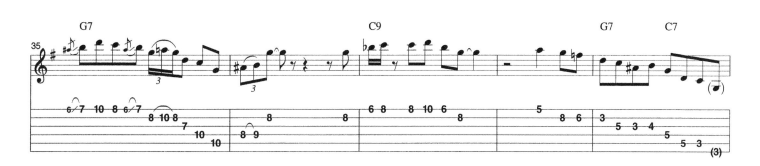

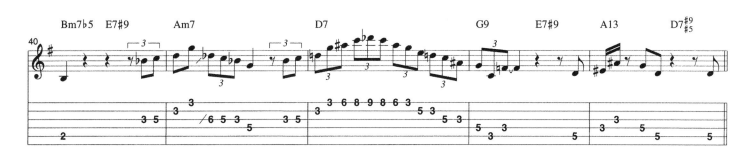

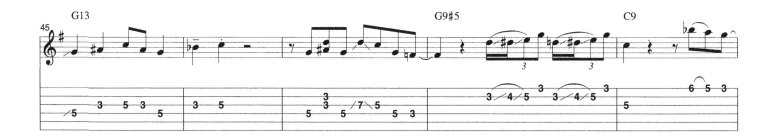

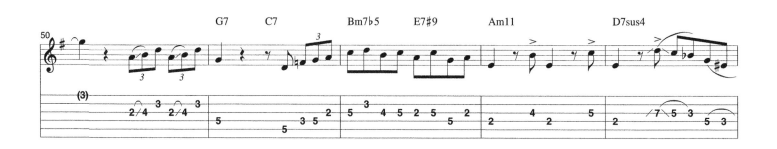

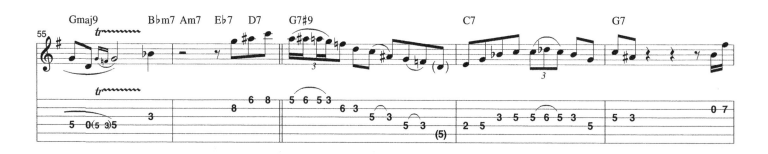

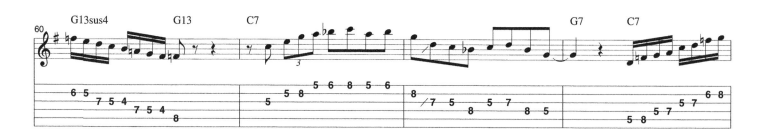

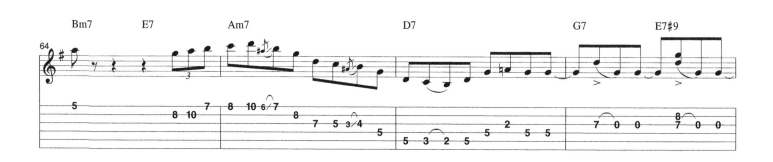

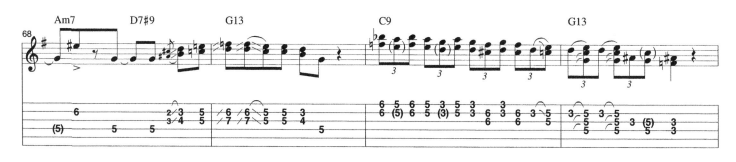

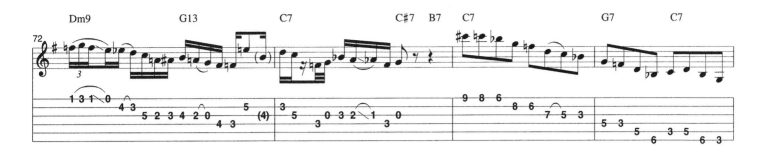

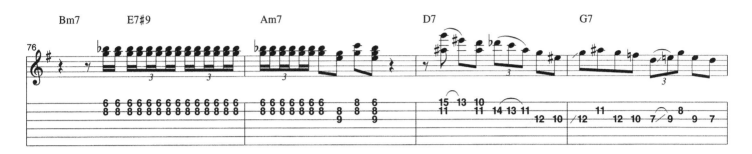

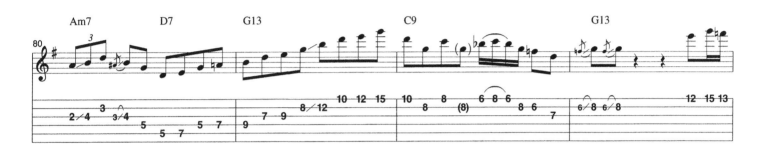

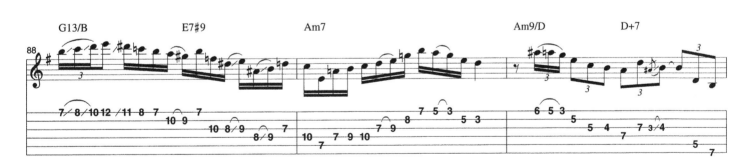

D Guitar Solo (John Pisano)

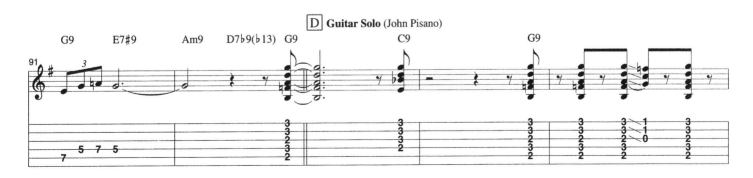

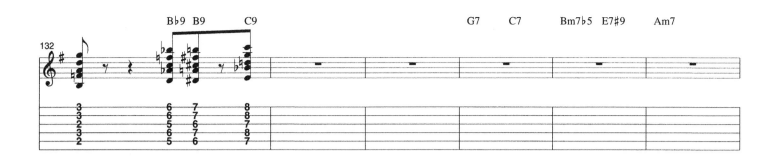

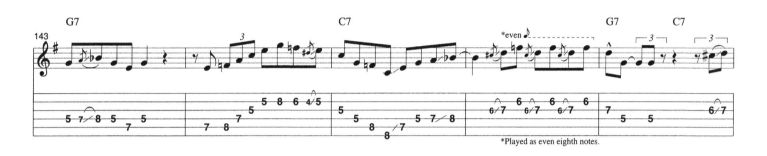

*Played as even eighth notes.

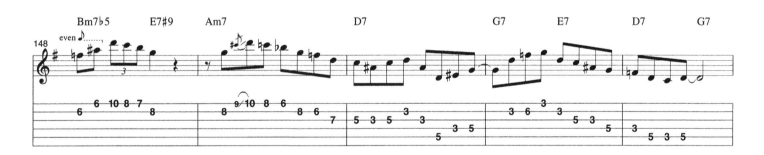

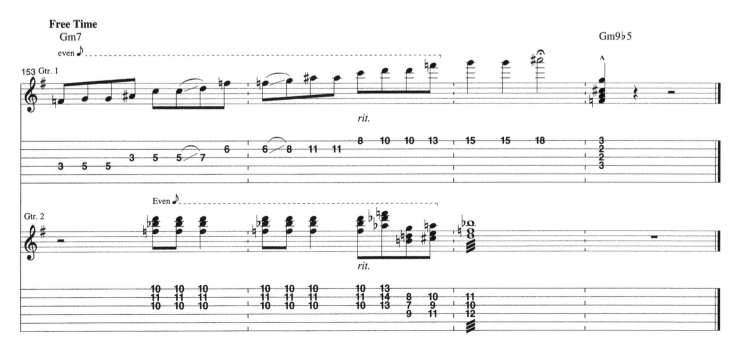

I Got Rhythm

Music and Lyrics by George Gershwin and Ira Gershwin

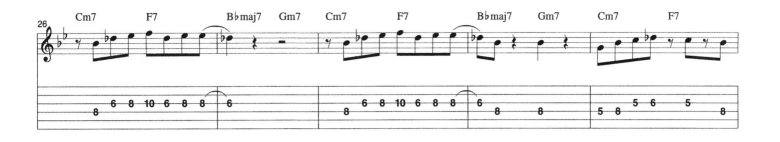

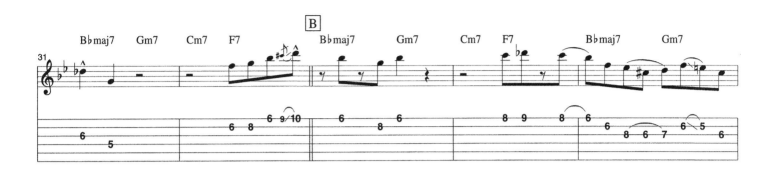

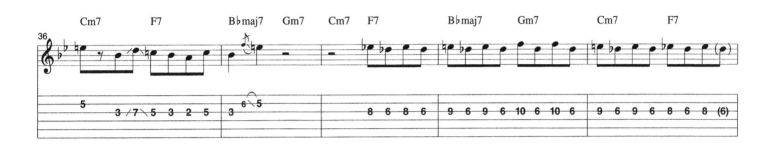

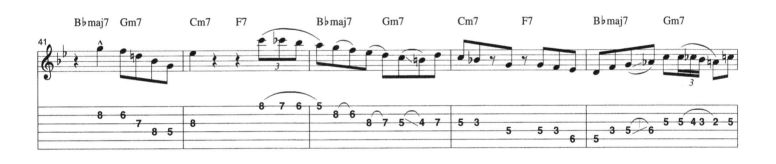

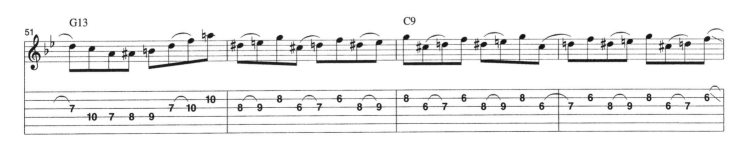

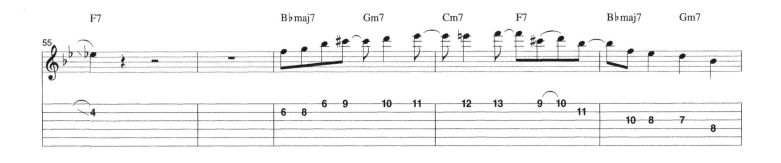

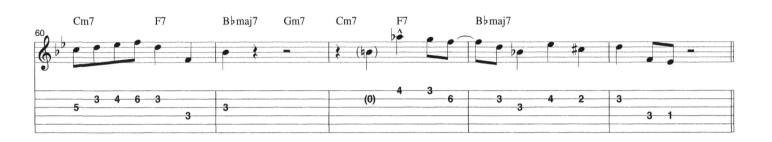

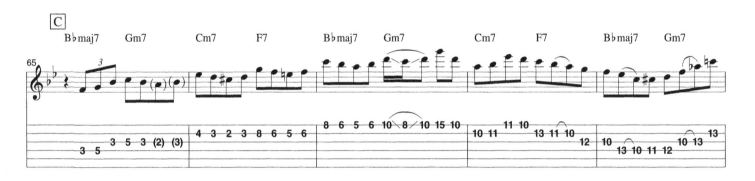

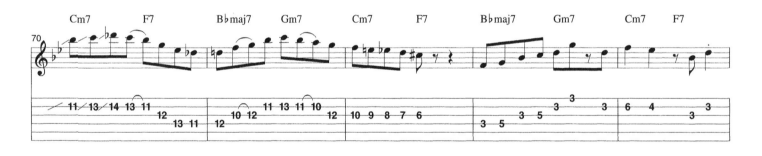

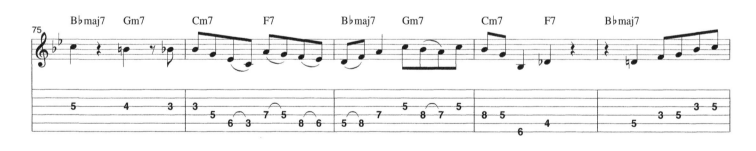

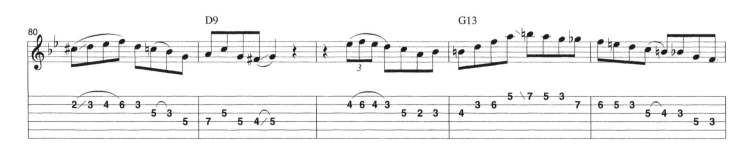

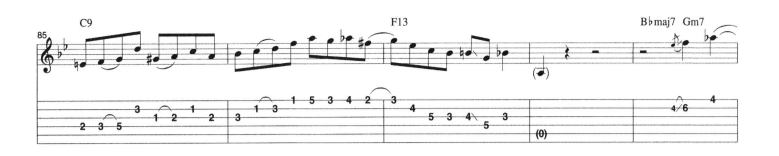

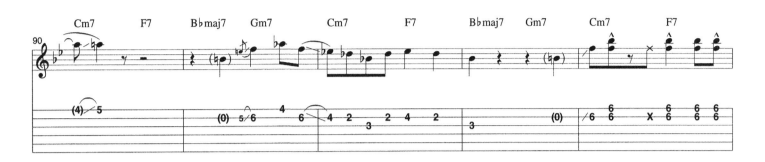

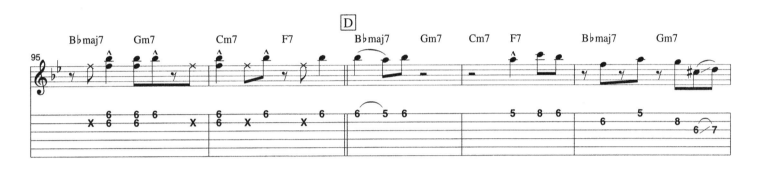

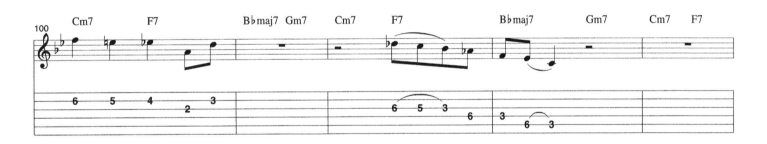

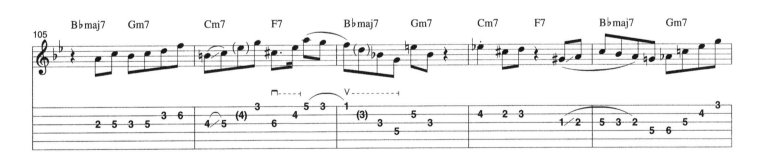

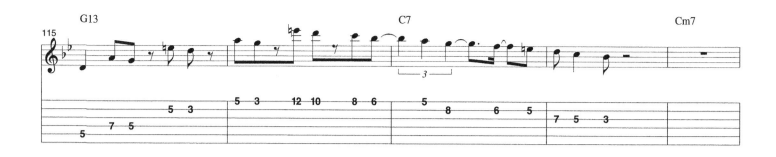

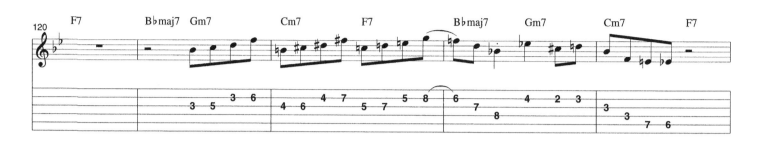

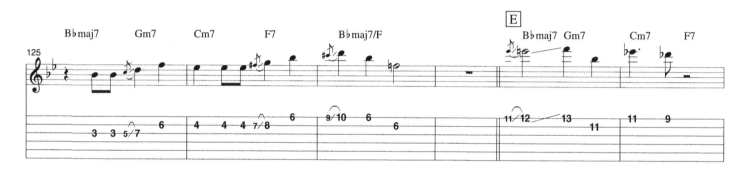

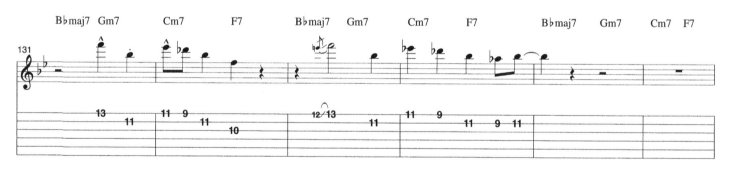

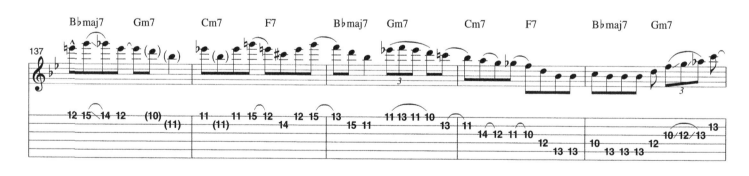

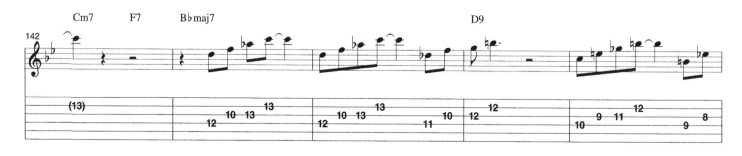

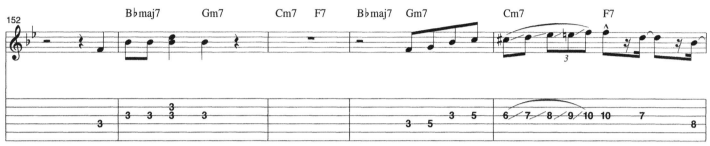

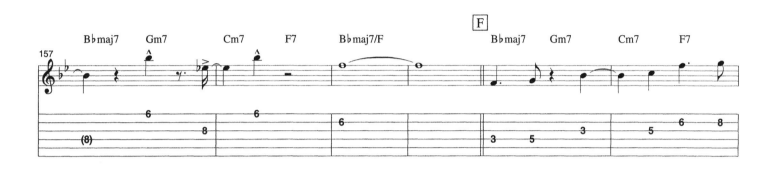

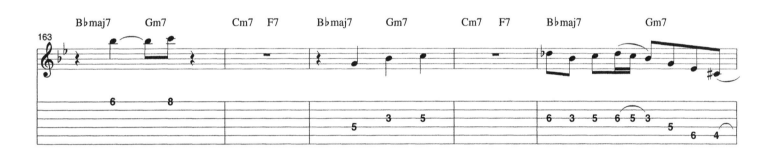

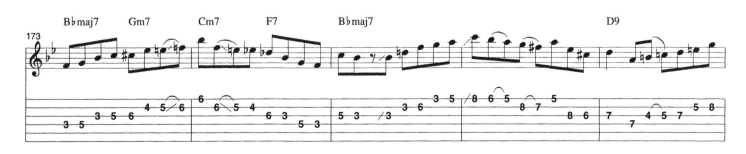

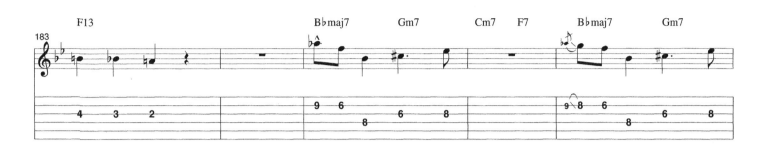

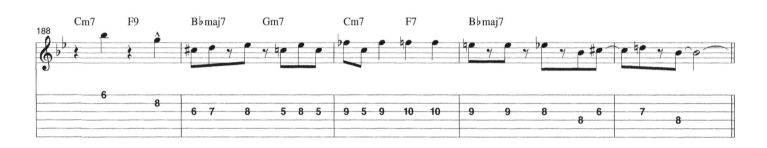

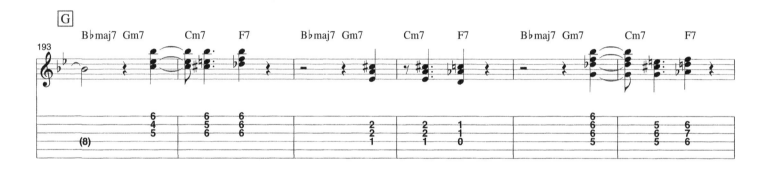

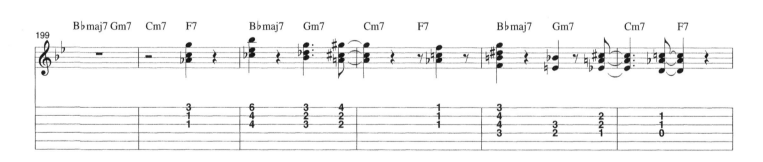

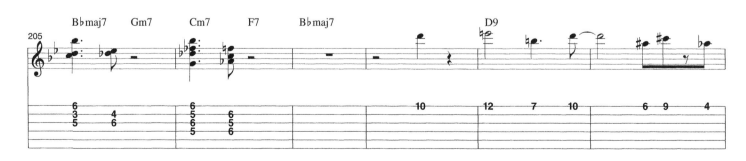

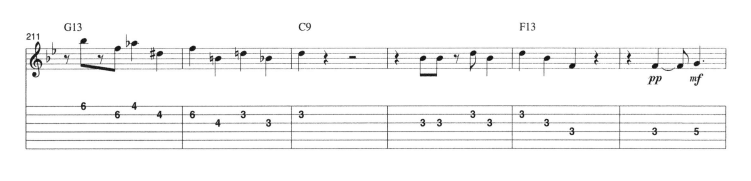

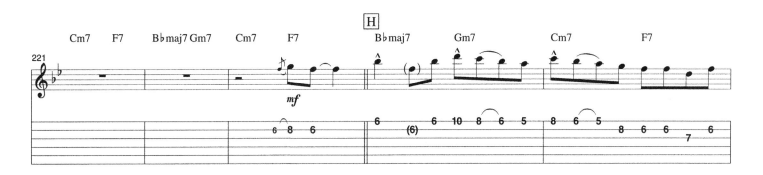

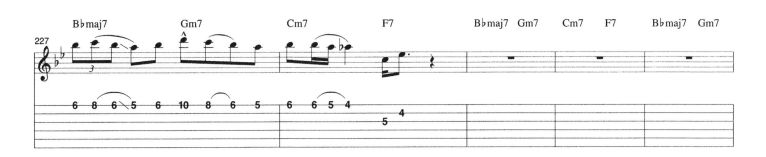

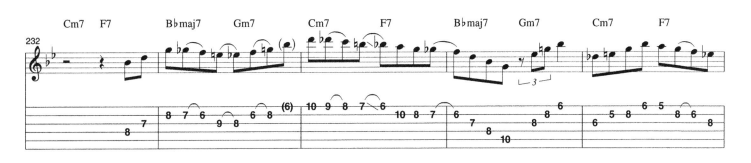

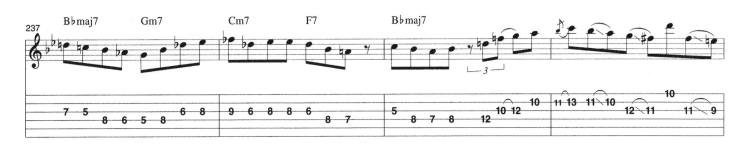

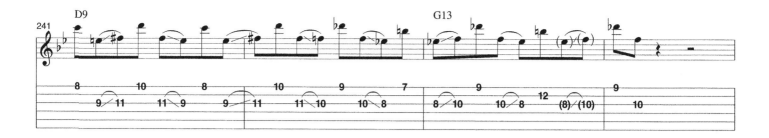

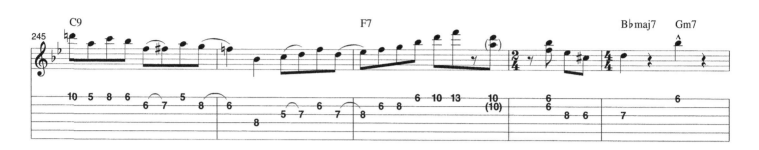

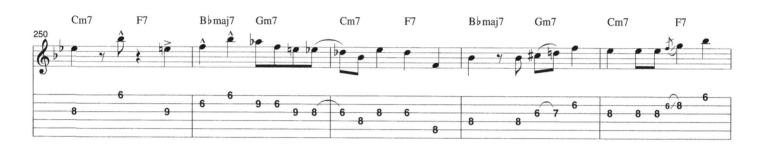

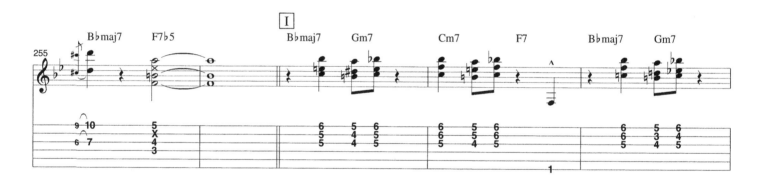

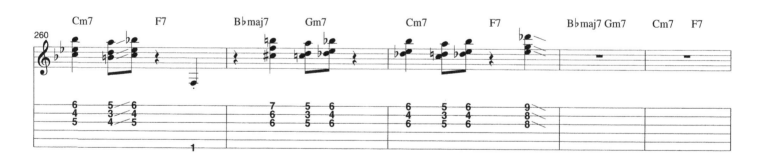

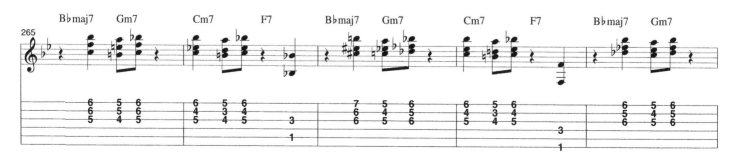

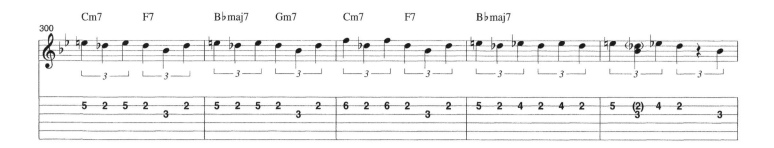

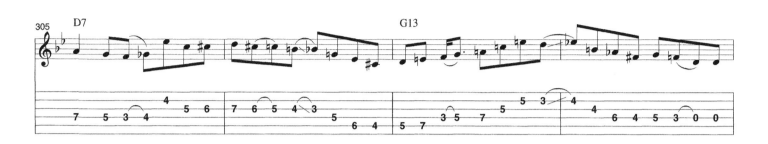

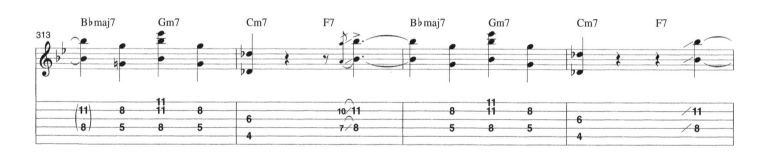

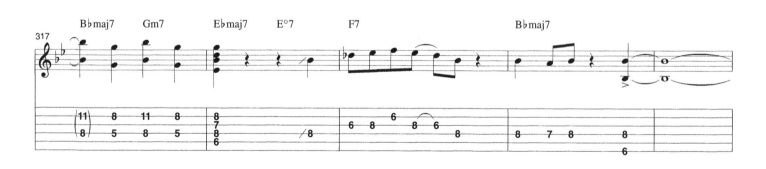

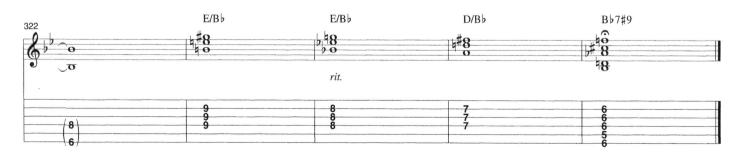

In a Sentimental Mood

By Duke Ellington

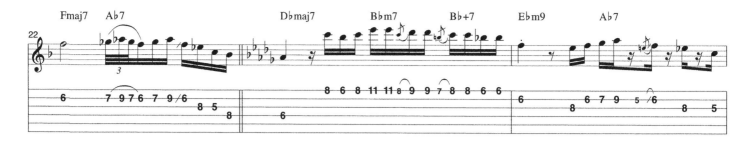

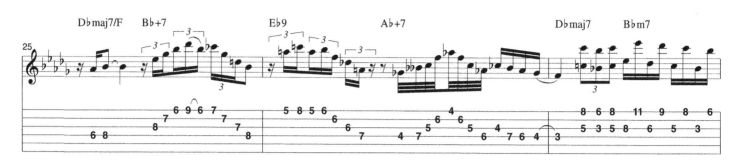

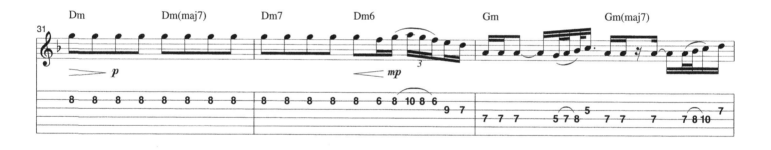

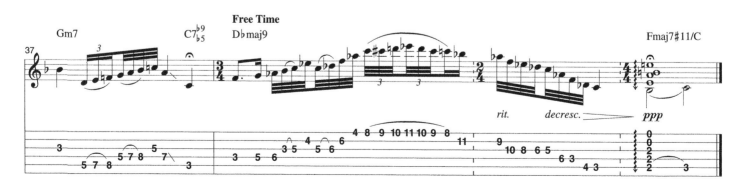

Pasta Blues

By Joe Pass

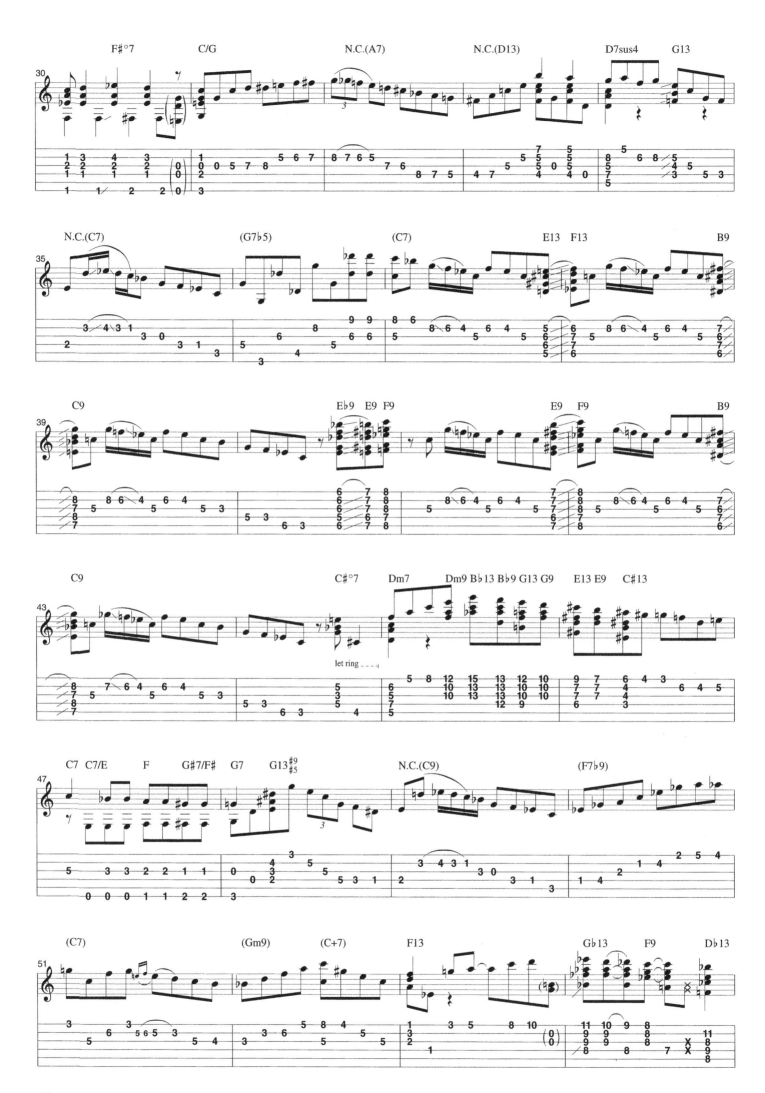

*Use pick-hand index and middle fingers to trem. pick.

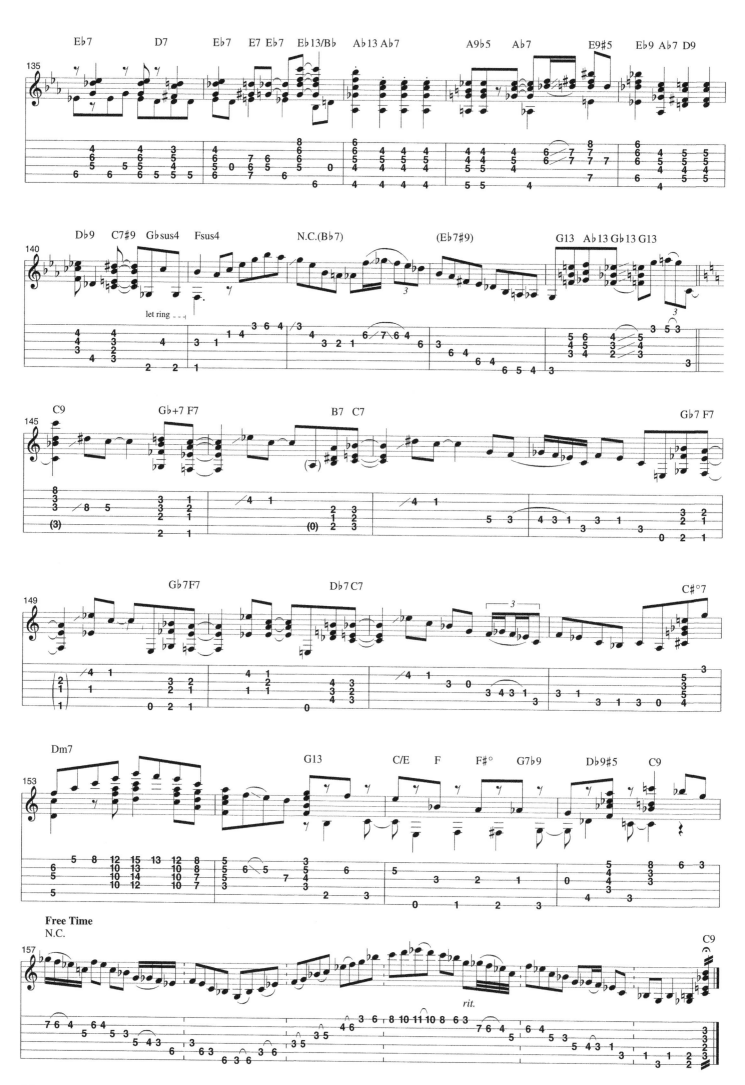

Satin Doll

By Duke Ellington

*Played behind the beat.

*Played ahead of the beat.

The Song Is You

Lyrics by Oscar Hammerstein II
Music by Jerome Kern

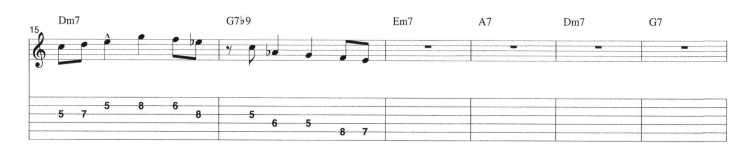

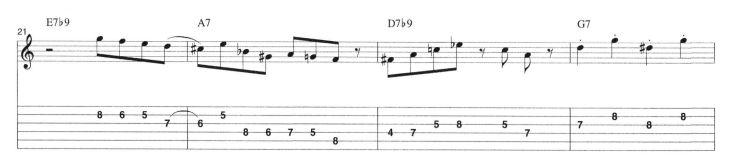

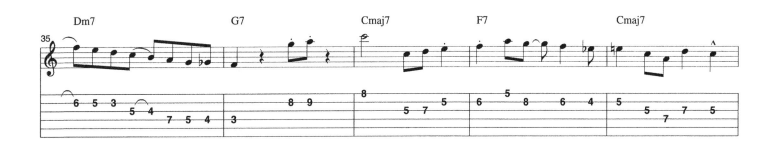

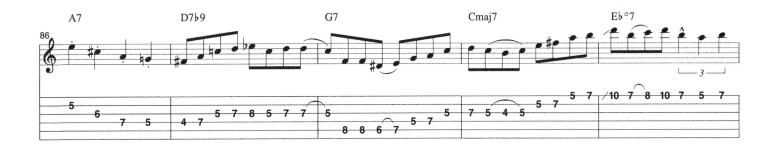

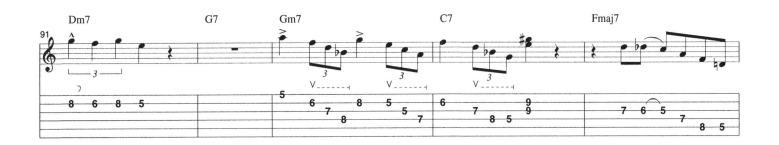

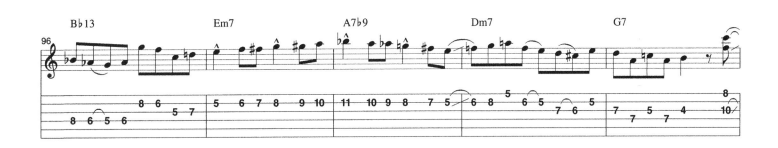

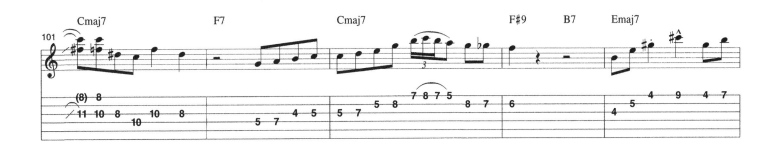

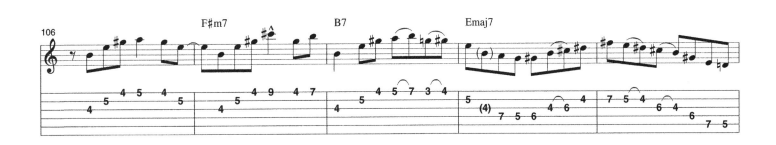

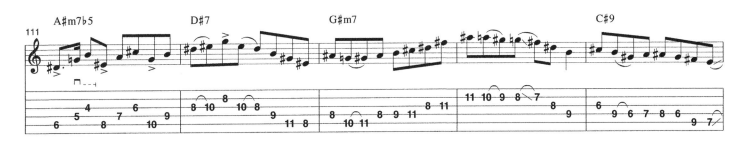

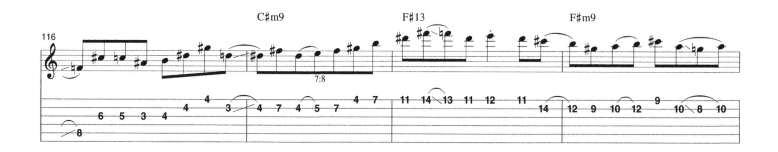

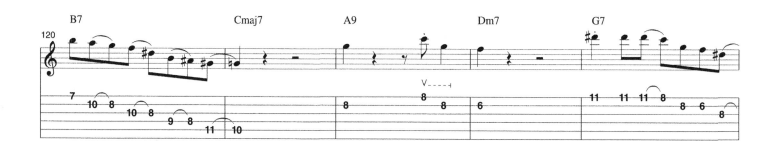

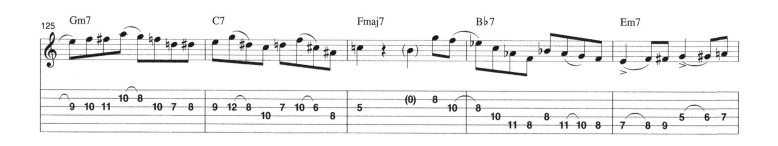

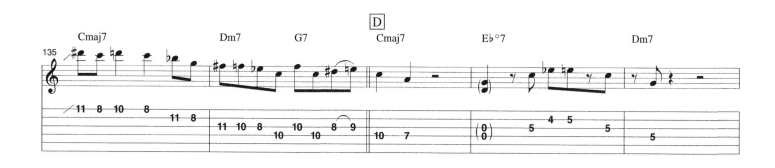

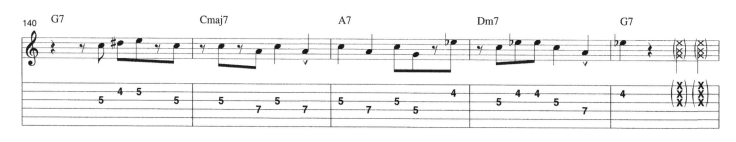

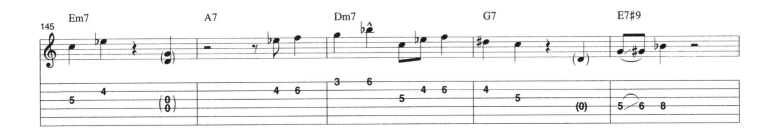

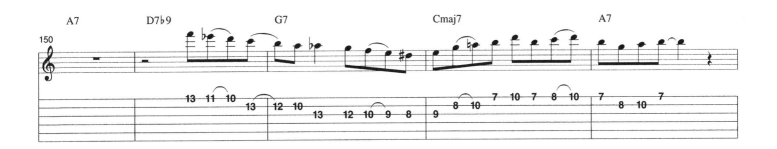

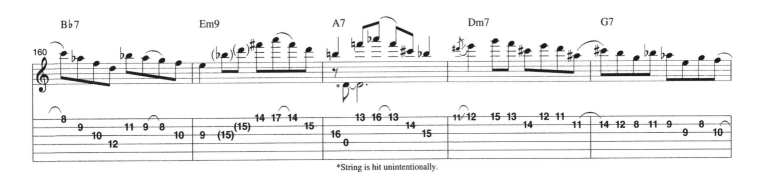

*String is hit unintentionally.

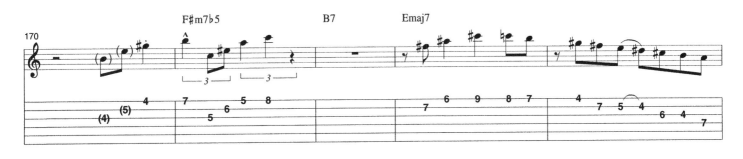

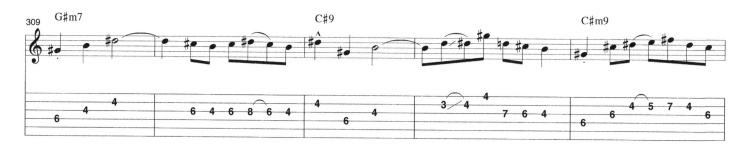

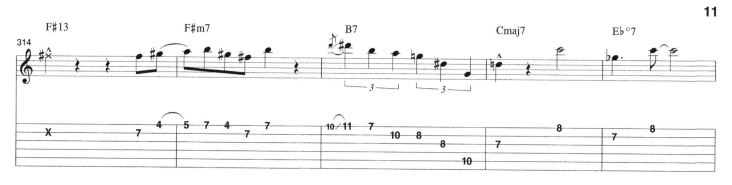

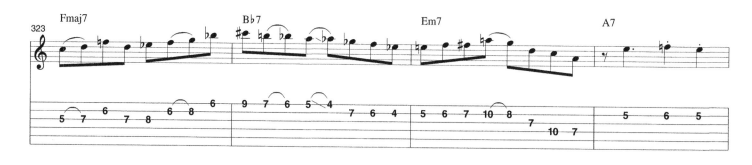

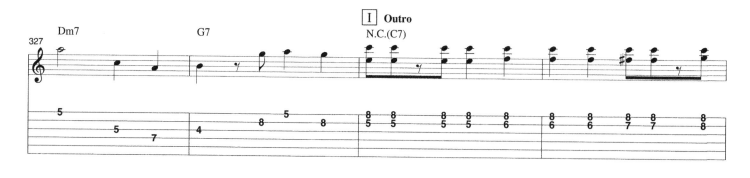

The Way You Look Tonight

Words by Dorothy Fields
Music by Jerome Kern

*Solo Gtr. Tempo fluctuates between 140 - 150 b.p.m.

*Lower note played ahead of the beat.

Yardbird Suite

By Charlie Parker

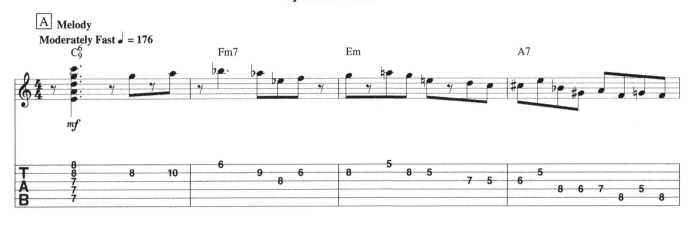

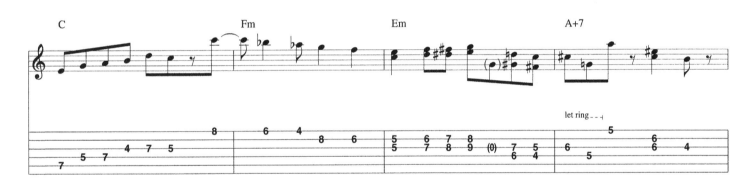

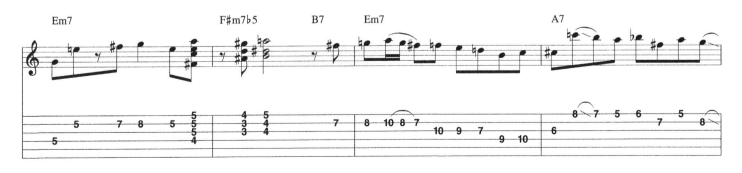

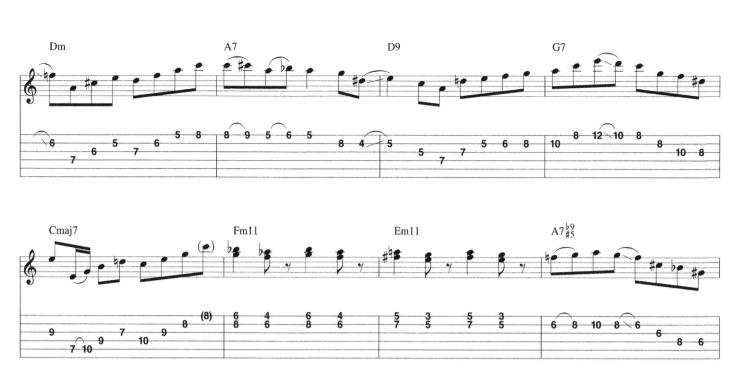

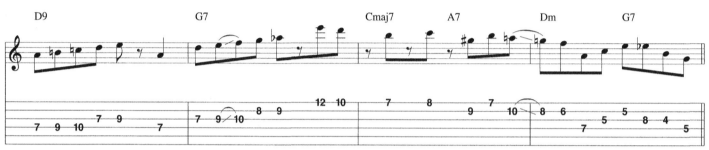

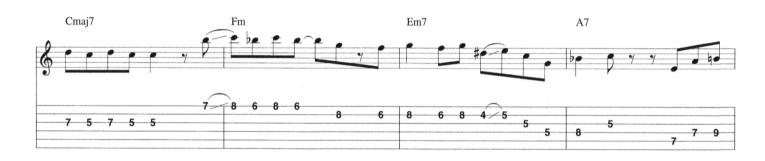

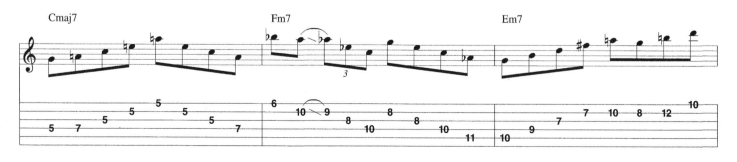

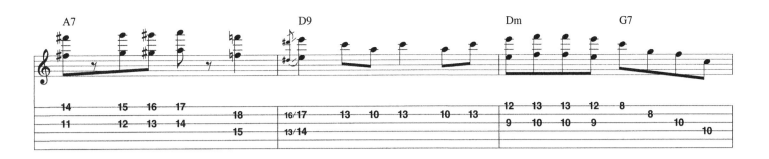

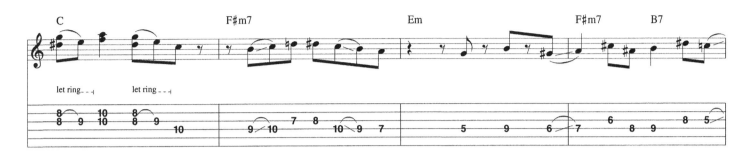

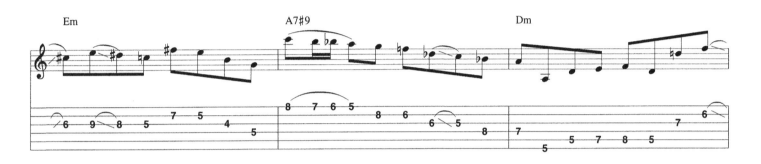

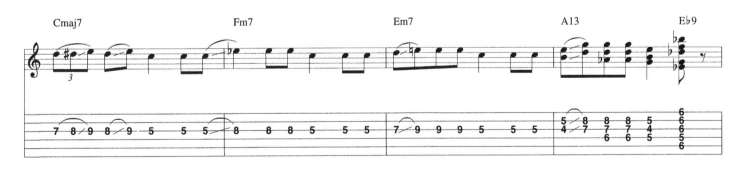

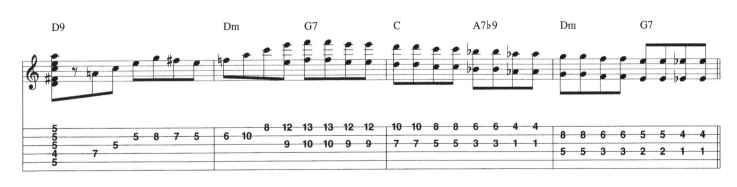

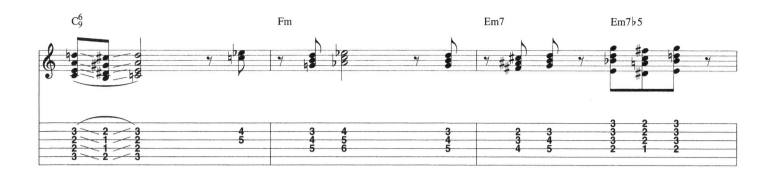

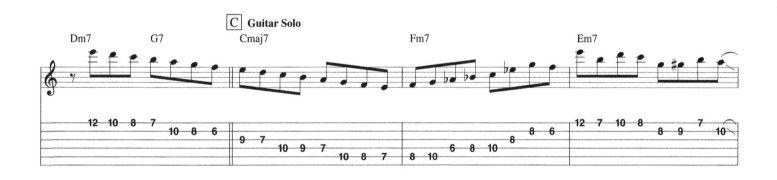

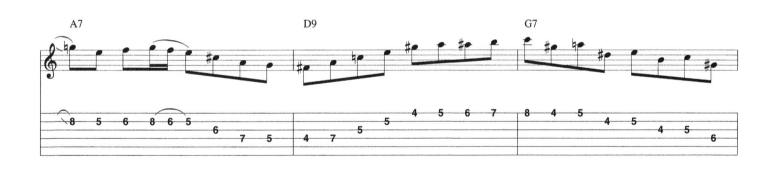

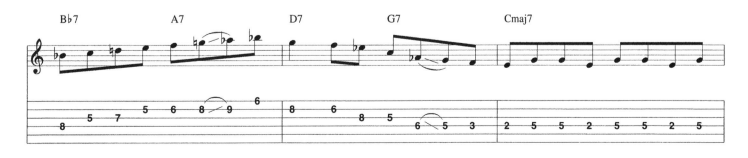

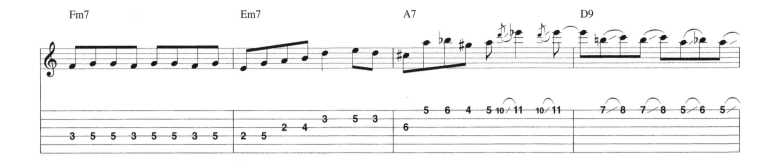

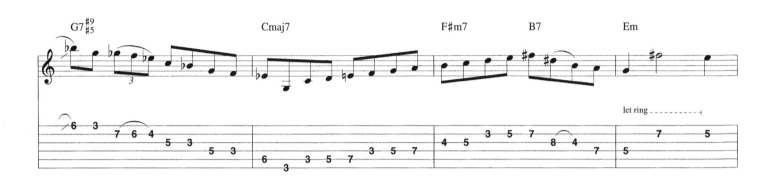

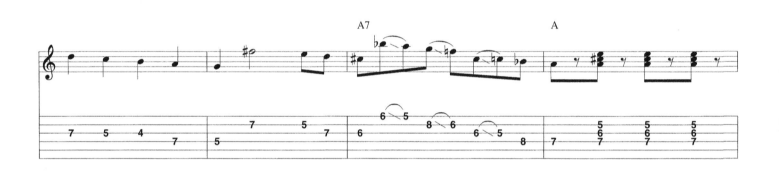

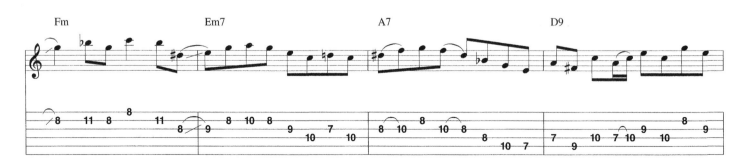

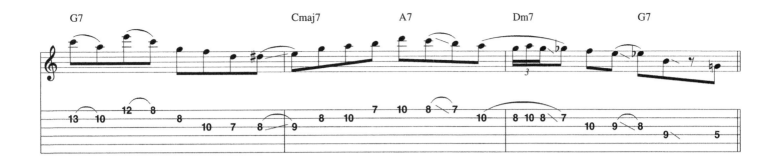

D Outro-Melody

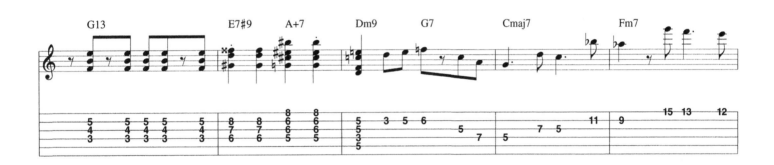

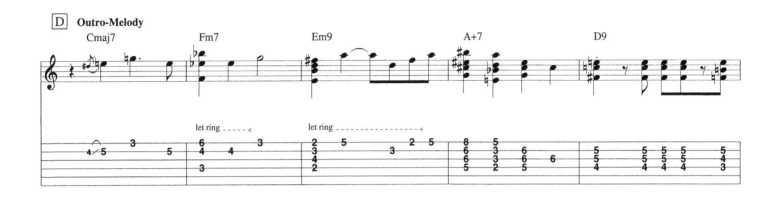

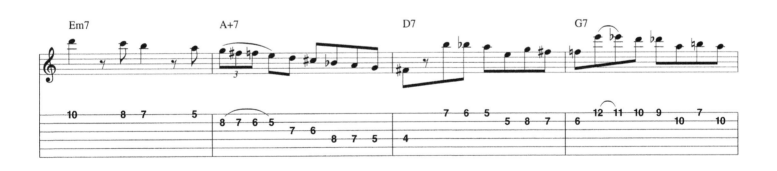

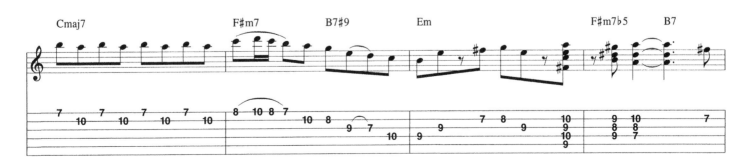

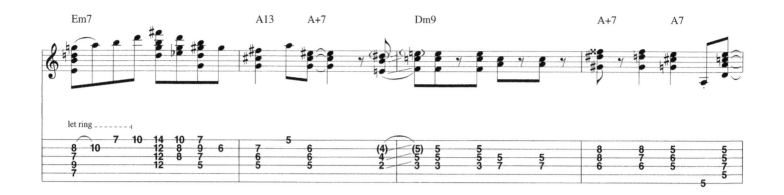

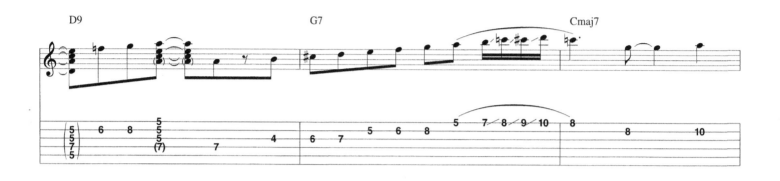

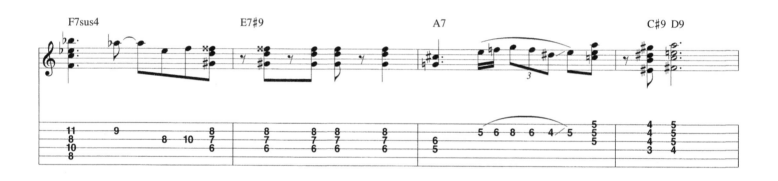